RESPONDING BIBLICALLY TO POVERTY, CORRUPTION, AND INJUSTICE

RESPONDING BIBLICALLY TO POVERTY, CORRUPTION, AND INJUSTICE

OKORIE KALU, DAVID LYONS, AND JOHN RIDGWAY

NAVPRESS

Discipleship Inside Out™

NavPress is the publishing ministry of The Navigators, an international Christian organization and leader in personal spiritual development. NavPress is committed to helping people grow spiritually and enjoy lives of meaning and hope through personal and group resources that are biblically rooted, culturally relevant, and highly practical.

**For a free catalog go to www.NavPress.com
or call 1.800.366.7788 in the United States or 1.800.839.4769 in Canada.**

ISBN-13: 978-1-61747-959-5

Cover design by Arvid Wallen
Interior design by Niddy Griddy Design, Inc.

Some of the anecdotal illustrations in this book are true to life and are included with the permission of the persons involved. All other illustrations are composites of real situations, and any resemblance to people living or dead is coincidental.

Unless otherwise identified, all Scripture quotations in this publication are taken from the *Holy Bible, New International Version®* (NIV®). Copyright © 1973, 1978, 1984 by Biblica, used by permission of Zondervan. All rights reserved. Other versions used include: the New American Standard Bible® (NASB), Copyright © 1960, 1962, 1963, 1968, 1971, 1972, 1973, 1975, 1977, 1995 by The Lockman Foundation. Used by permission; and *THE MESSAGE* (MSG). Copyright © 1993, 1994, 1995, 1996, 2000, 2001, 2002. Used by permission of NavPress Publishing Group.

Printed in Canada

1 2 3 4 5 6 7 8 / 16 15 14 13 12 11

CONTENTS

Introduction   7

Lesson 1
The Heartache of Man and the Heartbeat of God   10

Lesson 2
What Went Wrong and What Can Be Done?   19

Lesson 3
People Who Transform Communities   31

Lesson 4
Communities That Heal Relationships
    and Increase Justice   47

Lesson 5
The Nature of the Gospel of Jesus and
    His Kingdom   60

Lesson 6
The Gospel of Jesus and His Kingdom in Action   75

As you proceed through this study you will occasionally be directed to resources at www.respondingtoPCI.com. There you will also find a free editable PDF file of the entire study available for download, a forum for discussing issues and questions related to each chapter, and other resources. Access to that site is limited to those who are actually doing this study. The **Access Code** for the site is **PCIresources**.

INTRODUCTION

Somewhere deep in your heart there is a dream of the way things ought to be. You've felt it. It stirs in you when you see images of brokenness in the news; your heart cries out that life is not supposed to be like this. You may be feeling a little like Adam and Eve must have felt as they longed for how life had been before sin distorted everything. You have inherited a longing for a world unmarred by sin, poverty, corruption, and injustice.

Down through biblical history, the poets and prophets have reminded us of those longings and have called us to act on them. In this study, you will see this theme from Genesis to Revelation. In the Pentateuch, Moses will show you the way things were meant to be and what went wrong. Job and David and Solomon will draw you into the longings of God and man. The historical books will show you the successes and failures of ordinary people in responding to poverty, corruption, and injustice. The prophets will give you a painful look at what God has to say about that. Then we'll take a closer look at Jesus arriving and announcing the good news that the kingdom for which we all long has come near, demanding our response. Jesus announced His arrival this way:

The Spirit of the Lord is on me, because he has anointed me to preach good news to the poor. He has sent me to proclaim freedom for the prisoners and recovery of sight for the blind, to release the oppressed. (Luke 4:18)

So it is not enough to deliver the gospel to the doorstep of nations. We are called to advance the gospel of Jesus and His kingdom *into* our nations, where most people live in poverty and endure the effects of corruption and injustice. In 2003 the World Bank classified over 4 billion people as "poor" (living on less than $2 a day), while the five richest countries in the world receive 85 percent of the total world income.

As Jesus walked the earth, He treated every person with dignity and value, especially those who were not privileged or powerful. He demonstrated a heart for the whole person, and He showed compassion for the vulnerable and broken. He called us to nurture communities of faith and love that bring joy and hope to their surrounding environments as relationships are healed and justice increases.

This study was originally commissioned by international leaders of The Navigators seeking God's direction in how we are to respond to poverty, corruption, and injustice in the many contexts in which we live and minister. The authors[1] of the original study were Navigators from Nigeria, the Philippines, Ethiopia, Brazil, Australia, India, and the United States. So other Navigators should recognize the language of our calling, values, and vision throughout this study. It is our hope that every Navigator will recognize that responding to these issues is integral to what it means to be a Navigator. But our audience is not limited to Navigator staff. Everyone familiar with the Scriptures will also recognize these themes. In fact, here you will see that from Genesis to Revelation, responding to poverty, corruption, and injustice is central to being a good citizen in God's kingdom and living out His righteousness.

Some of the authors of this study grew up in poverty, yet each of us recognizes how we have somehow become blind to these biblical themes. Many evangelical believers can identify with that. But the Spirit of God is moving among His people, removing the scales from our eyes. May we become people who see.

---

[1]Okorie Kalu (Nigeria), Wency dela Viña (Philippines), Tsigereda Yemane (Ethiopia), Jairo de Souza (Brazil), Doug MacKenzie (Brazil/U.S.), John Ridgway (Australia/India), David Lyons (U.S./ International Ministry), and Bob Eschmann (U.S. Urban Ministry)

LESSON 1

THE HEARTACHE OF MAN AND THE HEARTBEAT OF GOD

(Your experience of this study will be enhanced if you watch Kit Danley share her story at www.respondingtoPCI.com.)[1]

What comes to your mind when you envision "the poor"? Do you think of a starving child in some faraway land? Or do you think of the homeless mother and her children you see along the way as you go about your business? The poor tend to be invisible to us, either because they seem far away or because we just don't see them anymore.

Whether the world would regard us as rich or poor, we need to become people who see. Kit Danley grew up in a wealthy, aristocratic family. Then her father killed himself and her mother collapsed into ugly, self-destructive behavior. Through all that, Kit began to

---

[1] Access Code: PCIresources

see the poverty in her own soul. And through her own poverty she met the One who says, *"Blessed are you who are poor, for yours is the kingdom of God"* (Luke 6:20, NASB).

In this chapter, we will take a closer look at three wealthy men who, like Kit, became people who see: Job, David, and Solomon.

From Riches to Rags: Job

God regarded Job as the greatest of all the men on earth in his day. (Job lived so long ago that many believe the book by his name is the oldest book in the Bible.) Why did God hold Job in such high esteem? There are many reasons, but the climax of Job's defense of his own righteousness focused on how he treated vulnerable and marginalized people.

1. **Read Job 29:12-17. List the kinds of people that Job helped and what he did for them.**

Job 29:12-17

I rescued the poor who cried for help, and the fatherless who had none to assist him.
The man who was dying blessed me; I made the widow's heart sing.
I put on righteousness as

> my clothing; justice was
> my robe and my turban.
> I was eyes to the blind
> and feet to the lame.
> I was a father to the
> needy; I took up the case
> of the stranger.
> I broke the fangs of the
> wicked and snatched the
> victims from their teeth.

Job loved the poor in practical ways, and apparently God loved that about Job. Ironically, the very man who may have been the greatest friend to the poor lost everything and ended up living among them in miserable poverty (see Job 1-2). He became so miserable that even the poor he had helped despised him (see Job 30:9). It was in this poverty that Job really got to know God as he had never known Him before (see Job 42:1-5).

From Rags to Riches: David

God found David working as a shepherd boy. He was one of "the least of these" in his family and his community. But God saw in David a heart He wanted to bless, and through the prophet Samuel, He announced that David would someday become king of Israel. As God began to move David toward the throne, the reigning king became jealous. King Saul tried to kill David, and David became a homeless refugee. Eventually Saul was killed and David was exalted to the throne, but he never forgot what it was like to be marginalized and vulnerable. That is part of what made him a man after God's own heart.

2. **As you look at these songs written by David and his friends, write down the kinds of vulnerable people that are mentioned.**

Psalm 10:17-18

You hear, O LORD, the desire of the afflicted; you encourage them, and you listen to their cry, defending the fatherless and the oppressed, in order that man, who is of the earth, may terrify no more.

Psalm 68:5-6

A father to the fatherless, a defender of widows, is God in his holy dwelling. God sets the lonely in families, he leads forth the prisoners with singing; but the rebellious live in a sun-scorched land.

Psalm 82:1-4

God presides in the great assembly; he gives judgment among the "gods": "How long will you defend the unjust and show partiality to the wicked? Defend the cause of the weak and fatherless; maintain the rights of the poor and oppressed. Rescue the weak and needy; deliver them from the hand of the wicked."

3. Go back and circle the words that describe what God does for the vulnerable. What do these words show you about God?

From Riches to Riches: Solomon

At the end of his reign, David anointed his son Solomon as king. Although Solomon was born into great wealth—and became perhaps the wealthiest man of his day—his writings suggest that he inherited some of his father's heart for the poor. More importantly, Solomon requested and received extraordinary wisdom right from the heart of God Himself. We have access to some of that wisdom through Solomon's writings.

4. **Solomon's wisdom led him to observe what happens to the poor. Read these proverbs and summarize Solomon's descriptions of how the poor are treated.**

Proverbs 13:23

A poor man's field may produce abundant food, but injustice sweeps it away.

Proverbs 14:20-21

The poor are shunned even by their neighbors, but the rich have many friends. He who despises his neighbor sins, but blessed is he who is kind to the needy.

Proverbs 14:31

He who oppresses the poor shows contempt for their Maker, but whoever is kind to the needy honors God.

Proverbs 19:1–9

Better a poor man whose walk is blameless than a fool whose lips are perverse.
It is not good to have zeal without knowledge, nor to be hasty and miss the way.
A man's own folly ruins his life, yet his heart rages against the LORD.
Wealth brings many friends, but a poor man's friend deserts him.
A false witness will not go unpunished, and he who pours out lies will not go free.
Many curry favor with a ruler, and everyone is the friend of a man who gives gifts.
A poor man is shunned by all his relatives— how much more do his friends avoid him! Though he pursues them with pleading, they are nowhere

to be found.

He who gets wisdom loves his own soul; he who cherishes understanding prospers.

A false witness will not go unpunished, and he who pours out lies will perish.

Proverbs 22:7

The rich rule over the poor, and the borrower is servant to the lender.

Proverbs 22:22

Do not exploit the poor because they are poor and do not crush the needy in court.

Proverbs 28:27

He who gives to the poor will lack nothing, but he who closes his eyes to them receives many curses.

Proverbs 29:7

The righteous care about justice for the poor, but the wicked have no such concern.

If you have read the story of Solomon's life, you may notice a problem here. As Solomon got older, he seemed to forget these lessons and became an oppressive ruler, building his wealth by taking advantage of the poor. Having wisdom is one thing; practicing wisdom is another. Knowing God's heart and ways is one thing; living in God's heart and ways is another.

The authors of this study are earnest about being doers of the Word, especially in our responses to poverty, corruption, and injustice. For some of us, that means helping extended family members find their way out of poverty. Others have taken initiative to feed hungry children in our community. Others are helping to liberate girls caught in human trafficking. Some of us have gone to battle with corrupt government officials who are not enforcing laws intended to protect widows and orphans.

5. **What are some practical responses to poverty, corruption, or injustice that you think God may have in mind for you and those close to you?**

LESSON 2

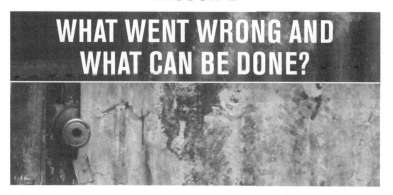

WHAT WENT WRONG AND WHAT CAN BE DONE?

(You can prepare your heart for this study by watching the stories of how The Navigators in Ethiopia are responding to poverty, corruption, and injustice at www .respondingtoPCI.com.)[1]

How did Africa become so poor? A casual observer might assume that Africans are lazy or unintelligent or that Africa lacks natural resources or is somehow cursed. But, by nature, Africans are just as hardworking and intelligent as others, and Africa is actually blessed with abundant natural resources.

So what has gone wrong? There are many answers. But any reasonable explanation must include the exploitation of Africa by colonial powers harvesting Africa's resources and imposing boundaries and systems that violate how tribes had coexisted before.

---

[1]Access Code: PCIresources

Even though colonial powers have withdrawn, the consequences of their rule continue to result in tribal violence and rampant corruption. It is estimated that corruption costs Africa $150 billion (U.S.) a year. That is 25 percent of the value of all that Africa produces each year in goods and services.

The corruption in Africa illustrates a global problem that afflicts our entire planet. To find the cause, we need to go back to the very beginning. God originally created an economy that worked well. In Genesis 1 and 2, He repeatedly described His creation as good, and when He was finished, He described it as very good. Everyone had enough, and everyone experienced justice.

But mankind disobeyed God and violated what He had set in place. Fractures have radiated throughout the whole system since then.

1. **As a result of Adam's disobedience, what changed about his work and his way of supporting himself?**

Genesis 3:17-19

To Adam he said, "Because you listened to your wife and ate from the tree about which I commanded you, 'You must not eat of it,'

(Note that Adam made his living from farming the ground.)

> "Cursed is the ground because of you; through painful toil you will eat of it all the days of your life. It will produce thorns and thistles for you, and you will eat the plants of the field. By the sweat of your brow you will eat your food until you return to the ground, since from it you were taken; for dust you are and to dust you will return."

Fast forward to today, a time when the news we hear about the world tempts us to turn away in despair or escape into our favorite TV show. But God did not give up and walk away. Listen to God's response: *"Into the hovels of the poor, into the dark streets where the homeless groan, God speaks: 'I've had enough; I'm on my way to heal the ache in the heart of the wretched'"* (Psalm 12:5, MSG).

Throughout human history, God has sent person after person to address the consequences of man's disobedience. We tend to look at people like Abram, Joseph, and Moses as "spiritual" leaders alone. But look at them again through the lens of God's response to poverty, corruption, and injustice.

2. What did God send these three men to do in response to poverty, corruption, and injustice?

Genesis 12:1-3

The LORD had said to Abram, "Leave your country, your people and your father's household and go to the land I will show you. "I will make you into a great nation and I will bless you; I will make your name great, and you will be a blessing. I will bless those who bless you, and whoever curses you I will curse; and all peoples on earth will be blessed through you."

How was Abram's presence on earth to eventually affect all the peoples on earth?

Genesis 45:4-7

Then Joseph said to his brothers, "Come close to me." When they had done so, he said, "I am your brother Joseph, the one you sold into Egypt! And now, do not be distressed and

What might have happened to Joseph's extended family if God had not sent Joseph ahead to Egypt?

do not be angry with
yourselves for selling
me here, because it was
to save lives that God
sent me ahead of you.
For two years now there
has been famine in the
land, and for the next
five years there will not
be plowing and reaping.
But God sent me ahead
of you to preserve for
you a remnant on earth
and to save your lives by
a great deliverance."

Exodus 3:7-10

The LORD said [to Moses],
"I have indeed seen the
misery of my people
in Egypt. I have heard
them crying out because
of their slave drivers,
and I am concerned
about their suffering.
So I have come down
to rescue them from
the hand of the
Egyptians and to bring
them up out of that
land into a good and

What did God see that
caused Him to send
Moses to Egypt?

spacious land, a land flowing with milk and honey—the home of the Canaanites, Hittites, Amorites, Perizzites, Hivites and Jebusites. And now the cry of the Israelites has reached me, and I have seen the way the Egyptians are oppressing them. So now, go. I am sending you to Pharaoh to bring my people the Israelites out of Egypt."

After delivering the sons of Israel from oppression, through Moses God prescribed a system of laws for His people. These laws were designed to minimize the destructive impact of man's unrighteous ways. Throughout these laws, God prompted His people to care for the vulnerable and oppressed.

3. **Read these laws given through Moses. Identify the vulnerable members of their society and what God told His people to do for them.**

Exodus 23:6

"Do not deny justice to your poor people in their lawsuits."

Exodus 23:9

"Do not oppress an alien; you yourselves know how it feels to be aliens, because you were aliens in Egypt."

Deuteronomy 10:18

He defends the cause of the fatherless and the widow, and loves the alien, giving him food and clothing.

Deuteronomy 24:14

Do not take advantage of a hired man who is poor and needy, whether he is a brother Israelite or an alien living in one of your towns.

4. These verses indicate that certain things tend to happen to these vulnerable groups of people. How do you see those same sorts of things happen in your society?

When we think of responding to poverty, corruption, and injustice, we tend to think only of our individual response. But God also called His people together to address oppressive systems in their society.

5. What systemic responses to poverty, corruption, and injustice do you find in these passages?

Deuteronomy 16:18-20

Appoint judges and officials for each of your tribes in every town the LORD your God is giving you, and they shall judge the people fairly. Do not pervert justice or show partiality. Do not accept a bribe, for a bribe blinds the eyes of the wise and twists the words of the

What was done for those who could not ensure that they were treated justly in the courts through their wealth?

righteous. Follow justice and justice alone, so that you may live and possess the land the LORD your God is giving you.

Leviticus 25:39-41

"If one of your countrymen becomes poor among you and sells himself to you, do not make him work as a slave. He is to be treated as a hired worker or a temporary resident among you; he is to work for you until the Year of Jubilee. Then he and his children are to be released, and he will go back to his own clan and to the property of his forefathers."

Deuteronomy 15:1-2

At the end of every seven years you must cancel debts. This is how it is to be done: Every creditor shall cancel the loan he has made to his fellow Israelite. He shall not require payment from his fellow Israelite or brother, because the LORD's time for

What was done for those who were trapped in bonded labor?

What was done for those who had become trapped in long-term debt?

canceling debts has been proclaimed.

It is unclear to what extent the Israelites ever put these laws into practice. Later in this study we'll look at how the prophets and Jesus rebuked the Israelites for their failure to respond to the poverty, corruption, and injustice around them.

Imagine how the Year of Jubilee would have impacted someone who had been living in hopeless debt. It would be like gaining one's life back and getting a fresh start.

How might that look today?

6. How might these commands be applied in a country in which godly people influence the system?

While preparing this study, at one point we met in Addis Ababa, Ethiopia. Over 90 percent of the people in that city live in vast slums in homes constructed of sticks and scraps of plastic and metal.

We spent a day with Dr. Jember, the "Mother Teresa" of Ethiopia. We saw how she and her people are giving Ethiopians their lives back, one block at a time. They organize the residents and help them tear down their huts. They provide the material and training to help them rebuild their block with concrete, plumbing, and hope.

We visited the People In Need Ministry, which rescues families of single mothers by providing education for one child in each family. That one will then be equipped to lead the entire family out of poverty.

We spent time with the Women at Risk ministry, which helps prostitutes learn practical skills so that they can build a new life.

Those who serve in these three ministries do all this in Jesus' name. And through them, many are gaining new life, both spiritually and practically.

7. **Think of the most vulnerable members of your community. What are some things that you and your friends might dream of being able to do for them in Jesus' name? How might this affect your ministry's strategic plans?**

LESSON 3

PEOPLE WHO TRANSFORM COMMUNITIES

(The lasting impact of this study may be enhanced if you prepare yourself by watching the movie "Amazing Grace," the story of William Wilberforce. You can get a free copy of the DVD at http://www.amazinggracemovie.com/)

We all have excuses: We're too busy. We're too young. We're not strong enough. We don't feel up to it. The problem is too big. We're not sure Christians should get involved in such things. William Wilberforce had all those excuses, but they did not stop him from investing his life in bringing an end to the slave trade that sustained the British Empire of his day. What set Wilberforce apart from others was that he listened to God's heart for the oppressed and responded without constraint from his apparent limitations.

John Wesley wrote to young Wilberforce, *"Unless*

God has raised you up for this very thing, you will be worn out by the opposition of men and devils. But if God be for you, who can be against you?"[2] Wilberforce stands tall in history as one who followed after God's heart in responding to poverty, corruption, and injustice. But he does not stand alone. In fact, he followed the example of many in the Scriptures who, through Christ, brought joy and hope to their surrounding environments and increased justice.

People Who Take a Stand

After Moses had led the Israelites out of oppression, he established systems of governing intended to prevent further oppression and injustice. Then he turned over leadership to his apprentice Joshua. Joshua led the Israelites from being a nation of refugees into a land of their own, and he laid foundations for them to become a model society. But after Joshua's death, things fell into chaos dominated by evil.

In those days there was no king in Israel; everyone did what was right in his own eyes. (Judges 21:25, NASB)

1. How did God respond to the evil chaos that prevailed after Joshua's death?

[2] http://www.forerunner.com/forerunner/X0554_Wesley_to_ Wilberforc.html

Judges 2:18

Whenever the LORD raised up a judge for them, he was with the judge and saved them out of the hands of their enemies as long as the judge lived; for the LORD had compassion on them as they groaned under those who oppressed and afflicted them.

We tend to think of the heroes of the Bible as merely spiritual leaders. But God devoted the entire book of Judges to a parade of everyday people who took a stand against evil and oppression in their community. Without an established government, most judges had to lead God's people into physical combat to restore order. Then the judge would rule over the people while maintaining justice. The greatest judge of the age was Samuel.

2. **How did Samuel's sons wander from the charter of what it meant to be a judge?**

> **1 Samuel 8:1**
>
> When Samuel grew old, he appointed his sons as judges for Israel.
>
> **1 Samuel 8:3**
>
> But his sons did not walk in his ways. They turned aside after dishonest gain and accepted bribes and perverted justice.

People Who Use Their Influence

Israel eventually tired of being ruled by judges and asked God to give them a king like their neighboring nations. Some of their kings were righteous and effective, while others just lived for themselves. This is true of leaders in every nation, city, community, tribe, and family.

3. How do righteous leaders affect those under their influence?

> **Proverbs 28:28**
>
> When the wicked rise to power, people go into hiding; but when the wicked perish, the righteous thrive.

Proverbs 29:2

When the righteous thrive, the people rejoice; when the wicked rule, the people groan.

Proverbs 29:4

By justice a king gives a country stability, but one who is greedy for bribes tears it down.

Proverbs 29:14

If a king judges the poor with fairness, his throne will always be secure.

Many modern societies have given greater influence to everyday people: those who vote, who lead businesses or institutions, who lead their tribe or clan, or who see needs around them and take the lead in responding to them. Few of us find ourselves at the top of society, or at the bottom. Most of us live somewhere in the middle—under the leadership of those above us while at the same time responsible for leading and serving others. Each of us is responsible for how we use the influence given to us.

4. Match the name of the person on the left with the description of his or her contribution.

People Who Used Their Influence	Their Contribution
1 Kings 3:16-28 Now two prostitutes came to [Solomon] and stood before him. One of them said, "My lord, this woman and I live in the same house. I had a baby while she was there with me. The third day after my child was born, this woman also had a baby. We were alone; there was no one in the house but the two of us. During the night this woman's son died because she lay on him. So she got up in the middle of the night and took my son from my side while I your servant was asleep. She put him by her breast and put her	Took a big personal risk to prevent violence and oppression. Mediated disputes so that the community would be stabilized by the hope that justice could prevail. Took initiative to help build infrastructure to protect the innocent and provide safe housing.

dead son by my breast. The next morning, I got up to nurse my son—and he was dead! But when I looked at him closely in the morning light, I saw that it wasn't the son I had borne." The other woman said, "No! The living one is my son; the dead one is yours." But the first one insisted, "No! The dead one is yours; the living one is mine." And so they argued before the king. The king said, "This one says, 'My son is alive and your son is dead,' while that one says, 'No! Your son is dead and mine is alive.'" Then the king said, "Bring me a sword." So they brought a sword for the king. He then gave an order: "Cut the living child in two and give half to one and half to the other." The woman whose son was alive was filled with compassion for her son and said to the king, "Please, my lord, give her the living baby! Don't kill him!" But the other said, "Neither I nor you shall have him. Cut him in two!" Then the king gave his ruling: "Give the living baby to the first woman. Do not kill him; she is his mother." When all Israel heard the verdict the king had given, they held the king in awe, because they saw that he had wisdom from God to administer justice.

Nehemiah 1:3; 2:17

They said to me [Nehemiah], "Those who survived the exile and are back in the province are in great trouble and disgrace. The wall of Jerusalem is broken down, and its gates have been burned with fire." . . . Then I said to them, "You see the trouble we are in: Jerusalem lies in ruins, and its gates have been burned with fire. Come, let us rebuild the wall of Jerusalem, and we will no longer be in disgrace."

Esther 4:13-14

[Mordecai] sent back this answer: "Do not think that because you [Esther] are in the king's house you alone of all the Jews will escape. For if you remain silent at this time, relief and deliverance for the Jews will arise from another place, but you and your father's family will perish. And who knows but that you have come to royal position for such a time as this?"

5. How did Nehemiah prepare to make a difference among his people?

Nehemiah 1:4

When I heard these things, I sat down and wept. For some days I mourned and fasted and prayed before the God of heaven.

Nehemiah 2:11-17

I went to Jerusalem, and after staying there three days I set out during the night with a few men. I had not told anyone what my God had put in my heart to do for Jerusalem. There were no mounts with me except the one I was riding on. By night I went out through the Valley Gate toward the Jackal Well and the Dung Gate, examining the walls of Jerusalem, which had been broken down, and its gates, which had been destroyed by fire. Then I moved on toward the Fountain Gate and the King's Pool, but there was not enough room for my mount to get through; so I went up the valley by night, examining the wall. Finally, I turned back and reentered through the Valley Gate. The officials did not know where I had gone or what I was doing, because as yet I had said nothing to the Jews or the priests or nobles or officials or any others who would be doing the work. Then I said to them, "You see the trouble we are in: Jerusalem lies in ruins, and its gates have been burned with fire. Come, let us rebuild the wall of Jerusalem, and we will no longer be in disgrace."

Change requires leadership, and leadership is basically influence. Solomon, Esther, and Nehemiah used their influence to affect policies and plans in their local and national situations.

6. **Are there any policies or plans in your local or national ministry that you could change to create a more effective response to poverty, corruption, or injustice? What are they?**

Everyday People Who Show Compassion and Defend the Helpless

It's easy to excuse ourselves from taking action because we don't have the kind of broad influence Samuel or Solomon had. So let's close this part of our study with an obscure farmer who showed compassion on a helpless widow.

Naomi had followed her husband to a land in which she was an unwanted minority. God blessed her with two sons who married local women. But a famine left them destitute. Then Naomi's husband and two sons died, leaving these three women as helpless widows. Naomi and her one daughter-in-law, Ruth, made their way back to Israel with nothing but the hope that the people there would help them because of the rules of compassion and justice written into the Law of Moses.

7. **How did the Law of Moses help the poor provide for themselves?**

> **Leviticus 19:9-10**
>
> "When you reap the harvest of your land, do not reap to the very edges of your field or gather the gleanings

of your harvest. Do not
go over your vineyard
a second time or pick
up the grapes that have
fallen. Leave them for the
poor and the alien. I am
the Lord your God."

Of course such laws were not always followed by
farmers who were either selfish or who thought of the
poor as lazy and unworthy. But Boaz was different.

8. **What do you observe about Boaz that set him apart
from the average farmer?**

Ruth 2:2-10

And Ruth the Moabitess
said to Naomi, "Let me
go to the fields and pick
up the leftover grain
behind anyone in whose
eyes I find favor." Naomi
said to her, "Go ahead,
my daughter." So she
went out and began to
glean in the fields behind
the harvesters. As it
turned out, she found
herself working in a
field belonging to Boaz,

who was from the clan
of Elimelech [Naomi's
deceased husband]. Just
then Boaz arrived from
Bethlehem and greeted
the harvesters, "The LORD
be with you!" "The LORD
bless you!" they called
back. Boaz asked the
foreman of his harvesters,
"Whose young woman
is that?" The foreman
replied, "She is the
Moabitess who came back
from Moab with Naomi.
She said, 'Please let me
glean and gather among
the sheaves behind the
harvesters.' She went into
the field and has worked
steadily from morning till
now, except for a short
rest in the shelter." So
Boaz said to Ruth, "My
daughter, listen to me.
Don't go and glean in
another field and don't
go away from here. Stay
here with my servant girls.
Watch the field where
the men are harvesting,
and follow along after the

girls. I have told the men not to touch you. And whenever you are thirsty, go and get a drink from the water jars the men have filled." At this, she bowed down with her face to the ground. She exclaimed, "Why have I found such favor in your eyes that you notice me—a foreigner?"

Some may wonder if responding to poverty, corruption, and injustice can really lead to spiritual generations. Isn't it interesting that Boaz ended up marrying Ruth, and their son became the grandfather of King David?

You may be thinking, "I'm not a Wilberforce, or a Samuel, or a Nehemiah." But you may be a Boaz, who simply shows compassion and takes initiative. You may be like one Navigator in Colorado who stepped in to help a homeless single mom find housing. Or you may be like a Kenyan Navigator who told his customers, "If you want to buy our GPS system for tracking your taxis, you'll need to pay your drivers a fair wage."

9. Which of the people in this chapter do you identify with? What do they inspire in you?

Don't limit yourself to thinking small. In 1955 Rosa Parks resisted injustice by refusing to give up her seat to a white man. Then Martin Luther King led a boycott and protests that eventually changed the way things are done in the United States. Nelson Mandela took a stand and suffered in prison for years — and eventually apartheid in South Africa was brought to its knees. Who will bring the exploitation of the caste system in India to its knees? Who will stop human trafficking? It will probably be everyday people making an extraordinary difference for the sake of the gospel!

LESSON 4

COMMUNITIES THAT HEAL RELATION-SHIPS AND INCREASE JUSTICE

In 1991, a white Navigator named Bob was given top-dollar tickets so that he could take ten African-American teens from his ministry to a professional baseball game. But when they arrived, they found their seats occupied by white men, and they were redirected to seats far in the back.

Later in the game, white security guards showed up and falsely accused one of Bob's friends of throwing things, insisting that they leave the stadium. As the group was leaving, a security guard pushed one of them down the stairs. When the teen asked why he had pushed him, the guard said, "Oh, you think you're a tough guy?" That teen was separated from the group in spite of Bob's objections. Thirty minutes later, he rejoined the group and told them how the guards had held him down while others punched him. Eventually Bob took his friends home.

1. **Imagine that you were Bob. What would you have been feeling as you went to sleep that night? What would you have done next?**

Bob contacted the general manager of the sports team, the local authorities, The Navigators, and a human-rights group. In each case, he persistently sought help to pursue justice. Ultimately, though, everyone he contacted failed to get involved.

Do you feel outraged? Do you feel like shouting at someone? Imagine this kind of injustice multiplied in countless situations around the world.

Now maybe you can understand the intensity of the Old Testament prophets. God was and is shouting about such things through the prophets. And He was especially upset with His own people.

2. **What injustices did the prophet Isaiah confront in these passages?**

Isaiah 3:13-14

The LORD takes his place in court; he rises to judge the people. The LORD enters into judgment against the elders and leaders of his people: "It is you who have ruined my vineyard; the plunder from the poor is in your houses."

Isaiah 10:1-2

Woe to those who make unjust laws, to those who issue oppressive decrees, to deprive the poor of their rights and withhold justice from the oppressed of my people, making widows their prey and robbing the fatherless.

There was a day when evangelicals viewed responding to poverty, corruption, and injustice as "social work" or a "social gospel" and mostly left it to "the liberals." But in 1974, Billy Graham convened the first Congress on World Evangelization, during which evangelicals affirmed the biblical unity of the social and spiritual implications of the gospel. The Lausanne Covenant stated:

> "We affirm that God is both the Creator and the Judge of all people. We therefore should share his concern for justice and reconciliation throughout human society and for the liberation of men and women from every kind of oppression."

Today the vision statement of The Navigators says that we envision:

> "Transformed communities . . . bringing joy and hope to their surrounding environments as relationships are healed and justice increases."

This is not a new vision. This has been on the heart of God since the dawn of creation. We think that we know God, but we have so much to learn about Him.

3. **Paraphrase what the prophet Jeremiah said about knowing God:**

Jeremiah 9:23-24

This is what the LORD says: "Let not the wise man boast of his wisdom or the strong man boast of his strength or the rich man boast of his riches, but let him who boasts boast about this: that he understands and knows me, that I am the LORD, who exercises kindness, justice and righteousness on earth, for in these I delight," declares the LORD.

Jeremiah 22:1-3

This is what the LORD says: "Go down to the palace of the king of Judah and proclaim this message there: 'Hear the word of the LORD, O king of Judah, you who sit on David's throne— you, your officials and your people who come through these gates. This is what the LORD says: Do what is just and right. Rescue from the hand of his oppressor the one who has been robbed. Do no wrong or violence to the alien, the fatherless or the widow, and do not shed innocent blood in this place.

Jeremiah 22:13-16

"Woe to him who builds his palace by unrighteousness, his upper rooms by injustice, making his countrymen work for nothing, not paying them for their labor. He says, 'I will build myself a great palace with spacious upper rooms.' So he makes large windows in it, panels it with cedar and decorates it in red. Does it make you a king to have more and more cedar? Did not your father have food and drink? He did what was right and just, so all went well with him. He defended the cause of the poor and needy, and so all went well. Is that not what it means to know me?" declares the LORD.

Imagine what God must think when He hears a comment like this from one of his followers, someone rushing home from church to watch a game on TV:

"Wasn't that great worship today? Now I'm ready to have a great day!"

Enthusiastic spiritual songs and awe-inspiring liturgies are wonderful, and they can be completely pleasing to God—when they are accompanied by a lifestyle of worship.

4. **According to the prophet Isaiah, what elements are essential to a life of worship that pleases God?**

Isaiah 1:15-17

When you spread out your hands in prayer, I will hide my eyes from you; even if you offer many prayers, I will not listen. Your hands are full of blood; wash and make yourselves clean. Take your evil deeds out of my sight! Stop doing wrong, learn to do right! Seek justice, encourage the oppressed. Defend the cause of the fatherless, plead the case of the widow.

Isaiah 58:6-7

Is not this the kind of fasting I have chosen: to loose the chains of injustice and untie the cords of the yoke, to set the oppressed free and break every yoke? Is it not to share your food with the hungry and to provide the poor wanderer with shelter— when you see the naked, to clothe him, and not to turn away from your own flesh and blood?

Prophets tend to make people uncomfortable. They notice what others overlook. They say what is on the heart of God as He reveals it to them without being too cautious about offending people.

5. **As the prophet Amos looked at the leadership of his nation, and especially at the judicial system, what was his evaluation?**

> **Amos 5:12-14**
>
> For I know how many are your offenses and how great your sins. You oppress the righteous and take bribes and you deprive the poor of justice in the courts. Therefore the prudent man keeps quiet in such times, for the times are evil. Seek good, not evil, that you may live. Then the LORD God Almighty will be with you, just as you say he is.

We might be tempted to think that this was just an Old Testament issue. But in Luke 4:18, Jesus quoted Isaiah 61:1-2 to describe His work on earth. This passage has both spiritual and physical implications. Those who first heard Isaiah, then Jesus, say these words probably saw the physical implications more easily. Today many of us tend to see the spiritual implications more easily.

6. **Read this passage and write down spiritual and physical things that Isaiah said the Messiah would do.**

Isaiah 61:1-4	Spiritual	Physical
The Spirit of the Sovereign LORD is on me, because the LORD has anointed me to preach good news to the poor. He has sent me to bind up the brokenhearted, to proclaim freedom for the captives and release from darkness for the prisoners, to proclaim the year of the LORD's favor and the day of vengeance of our God, to comfort all who mourn, and provide for those who grieve in Zion—to bestow on them a crown of beauty instead of ashes, the oil of gladness instead		

	Spiritual	Physical
of mourning, and a garment of praise instead of a spirit of despair. They will be called oaks of righteousness, a planting of the LORD for the display of his splendor. They will rebuild the ancient ruins and restore the places long devastated; they will renew the ruined cities that have been devastated for generations.		

The prophets Isaiah and Jeremiah, as well as Jesus, were speaking to a faith community of God's people, calling them to respond to poverty, corruption, and injustice in ways consistent with God's heart. God calls us to respond both as individuals and as a community.

One Community's Transformed Response to Poverty

In the early 1960s, the director of The Navigators of the Philippines noticed a trend that concerned him. Though they led university students to Christ and discipled them, many of them ended up leaving university early to support their families in faraway villages. This made it difficult to build a generational ministry year by year.

The needs of those students, along with a holistic understanding of the gospel, led the director to start a pig farm not too far from the campus to help the fruit of their ministry support students and their families.

However, other Navigators viewed the farm as a distraction, and asked, "Why do The Navigators raise pigs instead of laborers?" Unfortunately, the controversy eventually led to the resignation of the director.

Fast forward to 2004, The Navigators of the Philippines began planting small biblical communities all over the country among students, professionals, and families.

Two young brothers began regularly begging for food at the house where one of these communities met. At first the family was hesitant to give them food lest they foster dependency. But after three months, the family members asked, "What if God is the one sending the children to us?"

They began serving food in their garage every Sunday afternoon to more and more children and eventually to their families. Each meal started with teaching values and stories from the Bible. Students from the local campus ministry came to help and saw the holistic nature of the gospel at work.

As they developed relationships with the families of the hungry children, they began giving micro-loans to help them start businesses to support themselves. In other cases they helped to pay for the children's schooling. A multiplying movement of the gospel is growing there as a result.

This is the tale of one faith community in different seasons. Apparently Jesus has patiently been teaching these Navigators more about His heart and His ways.

7. As you review the words of the prophets, and as you think back over how God has been leading your faith community, what do you sense God may be saying to you and your friends?

LESSON 5

THE NATURE OF THE GOSPEL OF JESUS AND HIS KINGDOM

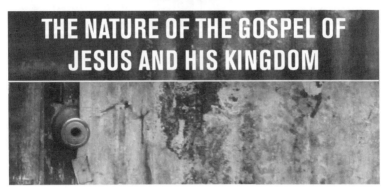

As a youth Doug helped to organize food drives and tutoring at a nearby orphanage. But when he began to walk with Christ through The Navigators' university ministry, he began to associate such things with liberal theology. He learned to think of social action merely as a way for people who didn't really understand the gospel of grace to feel better about themselves through doing good works. And he learned to spiritualize passages like Isaiah 58:10-12, believing they referred only to the spiritually hungry and spiritually oppressed.

If you spend yourselves in behalf of the hungry and satisfy the needs of the oppressed, then your light will rise in the darkness, and your night will become like the noonday. The LORD will guide you always; he will satisfy your needs in a sun-scorched land and will strengthen your frame. You will be like a well-

watered garden, like a spring whose waters never fail. Your people will rebuild the ancient ruins and will raise up the age-old foundations; you will be called Repairer of Broken Walls, Restorer of Streets with Dwellings.

Eventually Doug went overseas as a missionary and struggled as he was hit in the face with the poverty he saw. But he concluded that the best way he could help was by reaching university students with the hope that eventually the transformation of their lives would impact the poorer parts of their society. However, less than 10 percent of the people in this country have the opportunity to go to university, and over the years he noticed that the gospel was not trickling down to the poor through the students he reached.

Jairo was an exception. God had given him a heart for the poor, and he was asked to join the Navigator team that was shaping this study. Because Jairo did not speak English, Doug was asked to come along to translate. While Doug was translating, God began to open his eyes to His heart for the poor. From Genesis to Revelation, Doug was overwhelmed by God's compassion for the poor, the weak, the marginalized.

Over the years many students had asked Doug, "If God is just, why does He allow so much misery in the world?" And it struck Doug that God throws that question back to mankind. God has given *us* responsibility to take care of the earth. He has persistently urged *us* to care for those who suffer, and His pleas have often fallen on deaf ears.

Now Doug and his wife are actively responding to both the material and spiritual needs around them. They are seeing how the gospel of Jesus and His kingdom is designed to address the core of what makes the poor feel poor—an overwhelming sense of hopelessness and worthlessness. Now Doug sees responding to poverty, corruption, and injustice as integral to following Jesus as His disciple.

1. What do you identify with from Doug's story?

Resuming the Chant of the Prophets

Doug suffered from an inability to see, and he is not alone. This has characterized many of God's people down through the centuries. As we saw in the last study, God sent prophet after prophet to confront His people about their disobedience on these issues. Then God went silent for 400 years while His people were oppressed again, this time by Rome.

Finally God sent another prophet, John the Baptist, to prepare the way for the ultimate prophet: Jesus. Once again, John called God's people to repent. They responded by saying, "What shall we do?"

2. What did John the Baptist say to do to bring forth fruit in keeping with repentance?

Luke 3:10-14

"What should we do then?" the crowd asked. John answered, "The man with two tunics should share with him who has none, and the one who has food should do the same." Tax collectors also came to be baptized. "Teacher," they asked, "what should we do?" "Don't collect any more than you are required to," he told them. Then some soldiers asked him, "And what should we do?" He replied, "Don't extort money and don't accuse people falsely—be content with your pay."

By now this should sound familiar. These were the very sorts of things the prophets had been addressing for centuries. But John's primary role was to prepare the way for the prophet Jesus. And Jesus continued to confront God's people along similar lines.

3. **What important matters of the law did Jesus emphasize to the religious leaders of His day? What "camels" do you think they might have been swallowing?**

Matthew 23:23-24

"Woe to you, teachers of the law and Pharisees, you hypocrites! You give a tenth of your spices—mint, dill and

cummin. But you have
neglected the more
important matters of the
law— justice, mercy and
faithfulness. You should
have practiced the latter,
without neglecting the
former. You blind guides!
You strain out a gnat but
swallow a camel."

4. How did Jesus respond to injustice and lack of compassion in this passage?

Luke 13:10-17

On a Sabbath Jesus
was teaching in one of
the synagogues, and a
woman was there who
had been crippled by a
spirit for eighteen years.
She was bent over and
could not straighten
up at all. When Jesus
saw her, he called her
forward and said to her,
"Woman, you are set free
from your infirmity."
Then he put his hands
on her, and immediately

she straightened up and praised God. Indignant because Jesus had healed on the Sabbath, the synagogue ruler said to the people, "There are six days for work. So come and be healed on those days, not on the Sabbath." The Lord answered him, "You hypocrites! Doesn't each of you on the Sabbath untie his ox or donkey from the stall and lead it out to give it water? Then should not this woman, a daughter of Abraham, whom Satan has kept bound for eighteen long years, be set free on the Sabbath day from what bound her?" When he said this, all his opponents were humiliated, but the people were delighted with all the wonderful things he was doing.

John ended up in prison for confronting the immorality of Herod, and while there he began to have doubts about whether Jesus really was the expected Messiah.

5. **What did Jesus say to reassure John the Baptist that He was truly the one the prophets had predicted would come? Does His answer surprise you? How would this assure John?**

Luke 7:20-22

When the men came to Jesus, they said, "John the Baptist sent us to you to ask, 'Are you the one who was to come, or should we expect someone else?'" At that very time Jesus cured many who had diseases, sicknesses and evil spirits, and gave sight to many who were blind. So he replied to the messengers, "Go back and report to John what you have seen and heard: The blind receive sight, the lame walk, those who have leprosy are cured, the deaf hear, the dead are raised, and the good news is preached to the poor."

A New King and a New Kingdom

When Jesus assured John that "the good news [gospel] is preached to the poor," He was describing the gospel of the kingdom that He was teaching and preaching everywhere.

> *Jesus went throughout Galilee, teaching in their synagogues, preaching the good news of the kingdom.* (Matthew 4:23)

> *And this gospel of the kingdom will be preached in the whole world as a testimony to all nations, and then the end will come.* (Matthew 24:14)

The first thing we need to know about the gospel is summarized this way by Paul:

> *For what I received I passed on to you as of first importance: that Christ died for our sins according to the Scriptures, that he was buried, that he was raised on the third day according to the Scriptures.* (1 Corinthians 15:3-4)

Christ's payment for our sins, His death and His resurrection, are of first importance and foundational to all there is to know about the gospel, but it is not all there was to the gospel of the kingdom. Jesus went to great lengths to explain the nature of the kingdom that He was proclaiming. Many were hoping that Jesus would establish a new political kingdom to replace the oppressive Roman Empire. That caused a lot of confusion, and that confusion was part of what sent Jesus to the cross. But the kingdom Jesus was proclaiming was one in which people would live in obedience to the righteous rule of God. The King (Jesus) had arrived, and those who would surrender to His rule and authority would experience His kingdom. Jesus described His kingdom as something we can live in today:

As you go, preach this message: The kingdom of heaven is near. (Matthew 10:7)

When Jesus saw that he had answered wisely, he said to him, "You are not far from the kingdom of God." (Mark 12:34)

In reply Jesus declared, "I tell you the truth, no one can see the kingdom of God unless he is born again." (John 3:3)

Once, having been asked by the Pharisees when the kingdom of God would come, Jesus replied, "The kingdom of

God does not come with your careful observation, nor will people say, 'Here it is,' or 'There it is,' because the kingdom of God is within you." (Luke 17:20-21)

Stories of the Kingdom

Jesus told many stories to help people understand the good news about His kingdom. While there are many facets to it, among the most prominent is the way the vulnerable are treated in Jesus' kingdom. Let's look at two stories that illustrate this.

6. **According to Jesus, on what basis will He sort out those who are living in His kingdom from those who do not belong to His kingdom?**

Matthew 25:31-40

"When the Son of Man comes in his glory, and all the angels with him, he will sit on his throne in heavenly glory. All the nations will be gathered before him, and he will separate the people one from another as a shepherd separates the sheep from the goats. He will put the sheep on his right and the goats

on his left. Then the King
will say to those on his
right, Come, you who are
blessed by my Father;
take your inheritance,
the kingdom prepared
for you since the creation
of the world. For I was
hungry and you gave me
something to eat, I was
thirsty and you gave me
something to drink, I was
a stranger and you invited
me in, I needed clothes
and you clothed me, I
was sick and you looked
after me, I was in prison
and you came to visit me.
Then the righteous will
answer him, Lord, when
did we see you hungry
and feed you, or thirsty
and give you something
to drink? When did we see
you a stranger and invite
you in, or needing clothes
and clothe you? When
did we see you sick or in
prison and go to visit you?
The King will reply, I tell
you the truth, whatever
you did for one of the
least of these brothers of
mine, you did for me."

Jesus told other stories to explain how one gets into the kingdom. But in Matthew 25, He was explaining what it looks like when someone is living in His kingdom.

Another time, Jesus confronted a religious leader about whether or not he was practicing the two great commandments from the Mosaic Law (See Luke 10:25-28):

    a. Love God with all your heart, soul, mind, and strength.

    b. Love your neighbor as yourself.

The religious leader asked the question that many of us ask in our hearts when we are confronted with our responsibility to love the vulnerable and marginalized: "Who is my neighbor?" Jesus used that question to unpack this vital aspect of living in God's kingdom. We think of our neighbors as the people who live on either side of us. But Jesus urges us to think more deeply about what it means to be a neighbor.

7. Based on what Jesus said, how would you describe what it means to love your neighbor?

Luke 10:29-37

But he wanted to justify himself, so he asked Jesus, "And who is my neighbor?" In reply Jesus

said: "A man was going
down from Jerusalem to
Jericho, when he fell into
the hands of robbers.
They stripped him of
his clothes, beat him
and went away, leaving
him half dead. A priest
happened to be going
down the same road,
and when he saw the
man, he passed by on
the other side. So too, a
Levite, when he came to
the place and saw him,
passed by on the other
side. But a Samaritan, as
he traveled, came where
the man was; and when
he saw him, he took
pity on him. He went to
him and bandaged his
wounds, pouring on oil
and wine. Then he put the
man on his own donkey,
took him to an inn and
took care of him. The next
day he took out two silver
coins and gave them to
the innkeeper. 'Look after
him,' he said, 'and when
I return, I will reimburse
you for any extra expense

you may have.' Which of these three do you think was a neighbor to the man who fell into the hands of robbers?" The expert in the law replied, "The one who had mercy on him." Jesus told him, "Go and do likewise."

It is Scriptures like these that opened Doug's eyes to more of a complete view of what it means to spread the gospel of Jesus and His kingdom. We dream of seeing workers for the kingdom, like Doug, next door to everywhere.

8. **Take a moment and respond to this lesson. Jot down your latest thoughts about what it might look like for you and those in your faith community to be workers for the kingdom where you live.**

LESSON 6

THE GOSPEL OF JESUS AND HIS KINGDOM IN ACTION

Cherry met The Navigators as a university student in Ethiopia. After graduating, she experienced a frustrating year looking for a job. One evening during that year she went out with her family for the evening. On the way home, one of the tens of thousands of prostitutes in Ethiopia approached a nearby car. She was so aggressive that everyone in the area noticed, including Cherry's family. That spawned a debate among her family members; they wondered why anyone would go into prostitution. Someone said, "Why doesn't she just get a job?" But Cherry objected. "How can you say that? I'm a college graduate, and I've been searching for a job for a year. What real chance does that girl have of getting a decent job?"

Cherry did eventually find a good job, but thoughts about that girl caught in prostitution plagued her.

Eventually she began to believe that those recurring thoughts may be from the Holy Spirit. It was difficult to share her thoughts with others because she knew that most people would never imagine trying to actually help prostitutes escape their bondage. Fortunately, she was in a strong discipleship group in which she felt safe sharing her recurring thoughts and growing burden for the girls of the street. It was customary within this group to do what the Scriptures say. So they began to pray with Cherry about her burden and to offer counsel and encouragement.

Soon God provided a friend with a vision for partnering with Cherry in some sort of ministry. As Cherry shared her emerging vision, the friend joined hands with her and the two began praying daily about the next steps to take. They prayed for months, because the next steps seemed so scary. Eventually they began driving the streets on Thursday nights to pray for the girls they saw. They enlisted more intensive prayer from their discipleship group on those nights.

Eventually God gave them the courage to stop and talk to one girl. They asked her if she'd like to come with them to have some tea. She asked, "How much will you pay me?" Cherry said, "I don't have money for you, but I have something much better." The girl sneered, "Are you Christians? I've heard that before, and I don't want any of it." That was not an encouraging start!

But they drove on and found another girl who was much friendlier. When they invited her for pizza, she said "OK!" and jumped right in the car. In the restaurant, the threesome drew uncomfortable stares, but they tried to ignore the staring and engaged in cheerful conversation.

In the coming weeks, Cherry and her friend continued to spend Thursday nights visiting these girls on the street. They learned to bring food and drink along to share in the car. Although the first girl remained hostile, she began inviting her friends to be there to meet Cherry. Over time trust began to build. They talked, shared, laughed, and cried together. Eventually girls of the street began to say to Cherry, "If you really want to help us, help us to find a job and a better place to live." And she did.

Cherry and her friends refused to go on with their lives and not share what they were learning from the Scriptures. They took some simple steps to address the needs right in front of them.

Kingdom Habits and Practices

Because Jesus sent His Spirit to live in us, the King now lives in His people, and He longs to live *through*

His people. We are the body of Christ today, and we should live as members of His body, seeing what He sees, feeling what He feels, and letting Him respond through us.

1. **What did Jesus see and feel as He walked among those who were broken and oppressed? As His body, what should we see and feel?**

> **Matthew 9:36**
>
> When he saw the crowds, he had compassion on them, because they were harassed and helpless, like sheep without a shepherd.

If Jesus' disciples were really listening, and if we've accurately understood the gospel of the kingdom He preached, then we should expect to see His early followers actively responding to poverty, corruption, and injustice.

2. **What habits and practices of the early church demonstrated that they were living in the kingdom in responding to poverty?**

Acts 2:45

Selling their possessions and goods, they gave to anyone as he had need.

Acts 6:1

In those days when the number of disciples was increasing, the Grecian Jews among them complained against the Hebraic Jews because their widows were being overlooked in the daily distribution of food.

Galatians 2:10

All they [the apostles in Jerusalem] asked was that we [Paul and Barnabas in Antioch] should continue to remember the poor, the very thing I was eager to do.

1 Timothy 5:16

If any woman who is a believer has widows in her family, she should help them and not let the church be burdened with them, so that the church can help those widows who are really in need.

Acts 11:27-30

During this time some prophets came down from Jerusalem to Antioch. One of them, named Agabus, stood up and through the Spirit predicted that a severe famine would spread over the entire Roman world. (This happened during the reign of Claudius.) The disciples, each according to his ability, decided to provide help for the brothers living in Judea. This they did, sending their gift to the elders by Barnabas and Saul.

Kingdom Principles

Paul and Barnabas took the famine-relief collection initiated in Acts 11 very seriously. They used it to further teach about how to live as the corporate body of Christ on earth.

3. **What is it about the poor Macedonians that inspired others in their response to the poverty and distress in Jerusalem?**

2 Corinthians 8:1-5

And now, brothers, we want you to know about the grace that God has given the Macedonian churches. Out of the most severe trial, their overflowing joy and their extreme poverty welled up in rich generosity. For I testify that they gave as much as they were able, and even beyond their ability. Entirely on their own, they urgently pleaded with us for the privilege of sharing in this service to the saints. And they did not do as we expected, but they gave themselves first to the Lord and then to us in keeping with God's will.

4. **What is the "equality principle" that Paul taught the disciples in Corinth?**

> **2 Corinthians 8:13-15**
>
> Our desire is not that others might be relieved while you are hard pressed, but that there might be equality. At the present time your plenty will supply what they need, so that in turn their plenty will supply what you need. Then there will be equality, as it is written: "He who gathered much did not have too much, and he who gathered little did not have too little."

It should not be surprising that the Macedonians and other members of the early church were living in poverty. After all, Jesus and the apostles proclaimed the gospel of the kingdom to the poor. But the gospel also transformed the lives of many who were rich.

5. **What special challenges did Paul urge Timothy to impress upon the rich?**

1 Timothy 6:17-19

Command those who are rich in this present world not to be arrogant nor to put their hope in wealth, which is so uncertain, but to put their hope in God, who richly provides us with everything for our enjoyment. Command them to do good, to be rich in good deeds, and to be generous and willing to share. In this way they will lay up treasure for themselves as a firm foundation for the coming age, so that they may take hold of the life that is truly life.

Soon the rich and the poor were melded together into one new entity, the church. James spoke to the challenges that come when the body of Christ preaches good news to the poor. He described our response to the poor as the real test of the authenticity of our faith.

Religion that God our Father accepts as pure and faultless is this: to look after orphans and widows in their distress and to keep oneself from being polluted by the world. (James 1:27)

6. **According to James, what are several practical ways that pure faith is revealed in response to "the least of these"?**

James 2:1-17

My brothers, as believers in our glorious Lord Jesus Christ, don't show favoritism. Suppose a man comes into your meeting wearing a gold ring and fine clothes, and a poor man in shabby clothes also comes in. If you show special attention to the man wearing fine clothes and say, "Here's a good seat for you," but say to the poor man, "You stand there" or "Sit on the floor by my feet," have you not discriminated among yourselves and become judges with evil thoughts?

Listen, my dear brothers: Has not God chosen those who are poor in the eyes of the world to be rich in faith and to inherit the kingdom he promised those who love him? But you have insulted the poor. Is it not the rich who are exploiting you? Are they not the ones who are dragging you into court? Are they not the ones who are slandering the noble name of him to whom you belong? If you really keep the royal law found in Scripture, "Love your neighbor as yourself," you are doing right. But if you show favoritism, you sin and are convicted by the law as lawbreakers. For whoever keeps the whole law and yet stumbles at just one point is guilty of breaking all of it. For he who said, "Do not commit adultery," also said, "Do not murder." If you do not commit adultery but do commit murder, you have become a lawbreaker. Speak and act as those who are going to be judged by the law that gives freedom, because judgment without mercy will be shown to anyone who has not been merciful. Mercy triumphs over judgment! What good is it, my brothers, if a man claims to have faith but has no deeds? Can such faith save him? Suppose a brother or sister is without clothes and daily food. If one of you says to him, "Go, I wish you well; keep warm and well fed," but does nothing about his physical needs, what good is it? In the same way, faith by itself, if it is not accompanied by action, is dead.

It is easy for the rich to lose sight of how their wealth is often sustained at the expense of the poor. (Keep in mind the World Bank's 2003 classification of more than 4 billion people as "poor" — living on less than $2 a day — while the five richest countries in the world receive 85 percent of the total world income. It is likely that most people who complete this study are rich compared to most of the population of the world.)

7. **Contrast the responses to poverty, corruption, and injustice that you see in these two passages:**

James 5:1-5

Now listen, you rich people, weep and wail because of the misery that is coming upon you. Your wealth has rotted, and moths have eaten your clothes. Your gold and silver are corroded. Their corrosion will testify against you and eat your flesh like fire. You have hoarded wealth in the last days. Look! The wages you failed to pay the workmen who mowed your fields are crying out against you. The cries of the harvesters have reached the ears of the Lord Almighty. You have lived on earth in luxury and self-indulgence. You have fattened yourselves in the day of slaughter.

1 John 3:16-18

This is how we know what love is: Jesus Christ laid down his life for us. And we ought to lay down our lives for our brothers. If anyone has material possessions and sees his brother in need but has no pity on him, how can the love of God be in him? Dear children, let us not love with words or tongue but with actions and in truth.

8. As you review this lesson, which kingdom habits, practices, and principles do you think the Holy Spirit may be prompting you to put into practice?

Learning to Practice Kingdom Life

With Jesus living in us, we can make a difference in our world. Jesus intends to answer the prayer "Your kingdom come . . . on earth as it is in heaven" (Matthew 6:10). He intends to answer it in and through us. Are you up for that? If so, let's work on planning our response.

9. **Review lessons 1–6 and write down any convictions that are being formed in your heart. In the next column, write down any applications that the Holy Spirit is prompting you to make. In other words, what has God shown you, and what is He asking you to do in response?**

Lesson	Convictions: What Has God Shown You?	Applications: What Is God Asking You to Do?
Lesson 1: The Heartache of Man and the Heartbeat of God (pages 10–18)		
Lesson 2: What Went Wrong and What Can Be Done (pages 19–30)		
Lesson 3: People Who Transform Communities (pages 31–46)		

Lesson	Convictions: What Has God Shown You?	Applications: What Is God Asking You to Do?
Lesson 4: Communities That Heal Relationships and Increase Justice (pages 47–59)		
Lesson 5: The Nature of the Gospel of Jesus and His Kingdom (pages 60–74)		
Lesson 6: The Gospel of Jesus and His Kingdom in Action (pages 75–91)		

10. **Finally, write down possible next steps that you intend to discuss with others in your faith community.** (This could be your household, your Bible study group, your church, business associates, social group, or any group in which you find spiritual partnership and accountability. Your next steps might be individual or corporate.)

We also encourage you to share and discuss your responses to this study with others who have been through it. You can do so at the PCI Forum at www.respondingtoPCI.com.)[1]

---

[1]Access Code: PCIresources

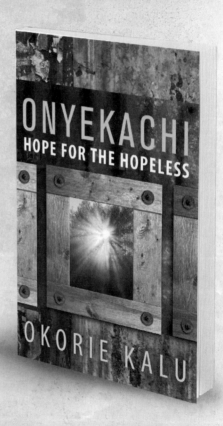